I Have Breast Cancer, Breast Cancer Does Not Have Me

CHERYL WILLIAMS

NEWMAN SPRINGS PUBLISHING
320 Broad Street
Red Bank, NJ 07701

First originally published by Newman
Springs Publishing 2024

ISBN 979-8-89308-656-0 (Hardcover)
ISBN 979-8-89308-657-7 (Digital)

Printed in the United States of America

DEDICATION

This book is dedicated to my beloved grandparents, Charles and Ethel Harris. They took a poor, directionless, misguided teen girl with no ambition other than to not live in the projects on welfare and food stamps and taught her how to become a lady. This had been my existence up until I went to live with them. My grandfather, whom I called Bigdaddy, always told me I could do better and that I could be whatever I wanted to be. He always encouraged me to get a college education. When I dropped out of college and got married at nineteen, I knew he was disappointed. He died when I was twenty-two. My grandmother only had a third-grade education, but she became a very successful entrepreneur who owned two very successful businesses. She became a cosmetologist and owned her own salon. When her health would no longer allow her to do this work, she learned floral designing and opened her own flower shop, which she operated until she retired. I learned my work ethic from her. I am forever grateful for their unconditional love and support. When my daughter was two years old, I went back to college. It took me ten years to finish my undergraduate work. I worked for AT&T full-time and went to school at night. I went back a few years later and earned my master's degree. I am sure my Bigdaddy is proud. It is no wonder that their life lessons were part of what motivated me to never give up when I was faced with the fight of my life with breast cancer.

I also dedicate this book to my daughter, Veronica, and my grand angel, Adriana. They have always been my motivation and what drives me to be an example of what you can accomplish if you work hard and persevere. I have always wanted more for them, wanted them to know the value of hard work and the satisfaction of accomplishing something you have worked hard for.

Lastly, I dedicate this book to my Lord and Savior, Jesus Christ, who has always sustained me. When I battled breast cancer, it was my faith that I held tightly to. God has never failed me.

ACKNOWLEDGMENTS

To my family and friends, church members, and sorority sisters who encouraged and supported me throughout this breast cancer journey, thank you.

A special thank you to one of my best friends for over forty-five years, Deborah Gray. Thank you for being there with me every step of the way. Thank you for asking the questions I couldn't even think to ask at the time and for praying for me.

Thank you, Edward, for supporting me during this time. You were very kind to me during this ordeal, and I appreciate you being an advocate for me.

Thank you, Sharlene Williams, for being a sounding board for me. As a breast cancer survivor yourself, you were always there for me and only a phone call away. Thank you for being my prayer warrior.

CHAPTER 1

My grandmother used to say, "A hard head will make a soft behind." It took me a long time to fully understand what that meant. It's sort of like trying to tell someone something for their own good, and they just don't get it. My daughter was like that when she was young. I could tell her not to bang her head on a brick wall because that would hurt. She would look at me, take a running leap at that wall, bang her head, and then turn around and say, "Ouch!" Well, I tried to tell her. You would think that in my late fifties, I would be beyond all those brick-wall moments, but not so.

For years, I have diligently gone for my annual mammogram and Pap smear. Many times, starting from my early thirties, I would have abnormalities on my mammograms. I remember the first time I was told to come back for a redo on my mammogram. It was unnerving. When they told me afterward that I needed to see a breast surgeon, I came undone! Waiting the weeks for the appointment was sheer agony. I went alone because I didn't want to accept that this could be something serious, and I wanted time to digest it by myself. When I met with the surgeon, she realized that what they had seen was a fatty cyst. She aspirated it in the office and sent me on my way. You can't imagine my relief! This same experience played out several times over the years, so much so that I no longer feared them. When I would be called back in, I would always go, but I also always felt like "Here we go again."

So in 2016, when I went for my annual mammogram and was told I needed to come back in six months because they thought they identified some calcifications, I told them my insurance didn't pay for mammograms every six months. I would see them next year. The first thing you need to know is my attitude toward the medical profession is less than complimentary. I have had so many experiences where it appeared the medical community was more interested in money than medicine. I saw it as an elite boys' club. They all had specialties so they could share patients. If you have one malady, they will share you with their friends so everybody can make money off the same patient. So I was not about to give them an additional opportunity to bleed my insurance company for more money. The second thing is I had never heard of calcifications. That word meant nothing to me, so it did not alarm me. Now, if they had said *lump* or *cyst*, maybe I would have paused for a moment. But nothing raised an alarm for me.

So right on time, the next year, I went back for my regular mammogram and was told that I would not be allowed to receive a regular mammogram because my chart had been flagged for diagnostics. *Diagnostics?* I was told that I needed to reschedule. I did so, thinking they were just trying to punish me for being a smart-ass and not coming back when they told me to. And so it started. The ordeal grew more tedious, tiring, time-consuming, and torturous as it went on. I endured the diagnostic mammogram (which didn't seem much different from a regular mammogram to me). From there, it was to see a radiologist, who confirmed calcifications. From there, it was an ultrasound and on to the dreaded biopsy. Now remember, I have seen this movie before. I was still thinking they were trying to scare me straight. However, after the experience of the biopsy, I started feeling like they were taking this crap a little too far! I can remember one procedure where they had me strapped face down on this table, trying to place a diagnostic dye in my veins. My uncooperative veins were really determined not to cooperate that day. This metal table was cutting me right underneath my breastplate. Oh yeah, and I was told not to move. After I had been strapped to this contraption of torture for about forty minutes, they finally realized they needed to get a nurse from the oncology lab. She is known as the port whisperer. She will come to play a very pivotal role in this saga as we go along. I had to lie still while this metal bar continued to press into my breastplate. When they got the dye in and finished the procedure, I was in so much pain I was in tears.

About six months before this ordeal started, I had just started dating a wonderful country man. I still had not let the thought enter my mind that this was anything other than the medical community flexing its medical muscle to teach me a lesson. However, Edward had recently been recovering from major surgery for the removal of one of his kidneys, which had been cancerous. He never mentioned the *C* word to me, but he remained glued to my side throughout this process like bread to the meat of a sandwich! When they finally released me from the torture table, I remember thinking that if I could just get to Edward, I would feel all better. He must have sensed my distress because he was pacing the floor outside the door and constantly looking through the window. As soon as I emerged, he burst through the door, and I collapsed in his arms in a meltdown mess of tears.

The next step was to see the radiologist and schedule a biopsy. Initially, the calcifications were identified in my left breast. After this biopsy, I was told I needed to have another one because the ultrasound seemed to show another area of calcification in the right breast too. She didn't have this info before the first biopsy. I had the second one done right after the first. Why the apparatus they use for this procedure has to resemble a medieval torture chamber is beyond me! Nothing about any of these procedures was easy! Now remember, I have had to endure some of this before when I have had to have various cysts aspirated. I am still back at "Y'all taking this punishment thing too dang far." At this point, I was told to just wait to hear the results of the biopsy. I expected a phone call that said I needed to see the surgeon again, and when I went, I would be told that they could aspirate another cyst. That is not the call I got.

CHAPTER 2

A day later, I got a phone call while at work. It was the oncology center at the women's breast cancer center. A soft-spoken female doctor said she was calling to give me the results of my biopsy. This time, as with each time I have faced these tests, when I heard the results, I felt like I was holding my breath. I was still not prepared for what I heard. After she said the *C* word, I don't think I heard anything else. My mind just went numb. I do remember my hands shaking and tears coming to my eyes. I heard something about HER2 positives or something negatives. The last thing I remember was her asking if I had any questions. I said no. I was really thinking, *Where do I start with the questions?*

I told my boss I was going to leave early and went home. After I sat with this news for a while, I called Edward. Only then did I start to cry. Only then did I realize I was scared. After we talked for a while and he prayed with me, I got myself together. I had to start thinking of a game plan.

For years, I have always believed that everything God allows to happen in my life is profitable to me for a reason. Often, what he allows me to experience is preparing me for the next matter in my life. Several years before this, one of my best friends experienced breast cancer. That was the first time anyone close to me had ever gone through breast cancer. I was recently retired, so I was not working. My friend is the kind of person who doesn't deal well with devastating news, so I ended up going to appointments with her and writing down information so she could absorb it later. She ended up having to undergo chemotherapy, a complete mastectomy, and radiation. I stayed overnight with her at the hospital after surgery, took her to her chemo appointments, and even picked out her new reconstruction boobs! This was a lengthy ordeal, but I was grateful that God had used me to be a blessing to her. So it occurred to me that God had allowed me to share this walk with my friend because I was going to have to walk this same road soon.

I had so much swirling around in my head. How was I going to tell my daughter and grand-angel? What was I going to do about my job? Also, Edward and I had only been dating a short while. This was too much to ask any man I had only recently started dating to deal with. I told him that I thought we should just take a step back for a minute while I dealt with this. I didn't want to impose on him, and I certainly did not want to ask him to attach himself to a woman dealing with cancer in the very early stages of a relationship. I didn't think it was fair. I certainly would not have blamed him if he said okay. I guess you know that's not what he said. This wonderful old country man said he was not going to leave me now while I was dealing with this. He recounted for me his ordeal with his cancer journey and said that the one thing he wished he had was someone by his side to be there for him during all of it. He said he would be there every step of the way for me.

I have always prided myself on being a strong, independent woman. I don't think I knew how much I needed someone by my side during this ordeal until then. Don't get me wrong. I had plenty of friends and family, but I just didn't want to be an imposition to anyone. Everyone has full, busy lives. I couldn't see myself asking anyone to put their lives on pause to hold my hand through this.

The first thing I had to do was keep the appointment they had set for me to meet with the oncologist. Edward and my best friend of over forty years, Deborah, both went with me. This appointment was about a week after the initial news. I had been thinking about this for a week. You know what I came up with? My mind told me that the name Cheryl Williams was a very common name and that they had gotten my chart mixed up with someone else's. Yeah! That's it. I was sure that when I went to my appointment, they would sort this out.

CHAPTER 3

When we arrived at my appointment, I met the oncologist for the first time. She was very nice, very thorough, and very detailed. She started talking about HR positives and HER2 negatives, meeting with the surgeon, chemotherapy, and radiation. The whole time, I was looking at her like she had two heads. She stopped talking and drawing briefly when she saw my expression and asked me if I was all right. That is when it dawned on me that she really was talking about me! I was speechless.

As I cried and Edward held my hand, Deborah started asking the questions that needed to be answered. "What stage? What are the options going forward? What is the prognosis?"

The doctor answered, and Deborah wrote down all the answers. I asked if I could just have a minute to gather myself. I went to the ladies' room. I looked in the mirror and cried for myself. I didn't say, "Why me?" I said, "Lord, why not me?"

After I sat there for a few minutes, prayed, and cried for a few more minutes, I wiped my face, put my big-girl panties on, and resolved to come up with a game plan. I went back into the room, and now I asked the questions. The first thing I asked for was an all-female team. So far, my oncologist and radiologist had both been female. Now they were telling me I needed to meet with a breast cancer surgeon, and I wanted a female for that too.

I am convinced of two things regarding this journey. One, you have the right and an obligation to proactively participate in your own health care. Two, you must have confidence in your health-care team. It was important to me that my health-care team be all female because breasts and hair mean something totally different to a woman than they do to a man. I am not insinuating that a male doctor cannot treat breast cancer, but I wanted to be assured that my doctor was treating me from both a medical and an emotional perspective.

I took the information Deborah had written down and went over it when I got home. I looked up some information online when I had questions, and I prayed. I also reached out to my friend that I had helped through this a few years earlier. She is a true prayer warrior, and I wanted to know mentally and spiritually how she dealt with this and what I could do. One of my sorority line sisters was also a long-time survivor, so I reached out to her too.

As women, we often get a bad rap for being petty and catty with one another. That has never been my experience, and these two women buffeted me on both sides. They listened to me, prayed with me, and supported me with whatever information they could impart to me. I learned that trying to maintain a positive mental outlook would aid in my healing process and that it was okay to admit when I was struggling.

That was beneficial to me because I was used to always being Superwoman. I'm the oldest child, so I was the one looking out for my siblings. I was the one who always took charge and got things done. I was the one who organized the reunions and planned the funerals. I was the one who donated a kidney. I was the one who made sure to lead by example. Now I was the one uncertain about how to navigate these waters. However, I was certain of one thing: cancer had picked a fight with the wrong woman!

CHAPTER 4

With my new resolve, I got busy planning my work in preparation for working my plan. I met with a wonderful breast cancer surgeon who came highly recommended. Everyone at Vanderbilt spoke about how smart and thorough she was. As it turned out, she remembered me. She had graduated high school with my daughter! We discussed a game plan. She wanted to review my chart again, and we would talk again afterward.

At my next appointment, both she and my oncologist were there. It appeared that the intensity of the calcifications might require a mastectomy of my left breast. It turned out the right breast was fine. I would need to undergo chemo and radiation. It was recommended that I take four chemo drugs that would be administered every three weeks. You need to understand my level of hysterics at this point. Through wails, I tried to explain that my "make-me-feel-better store" was Victoria's Secret. I always went to shop for bras and panties whenever I needed a pick-me-up. How in the world was I going to be able to shop at Victoria's Secret with one breast! Dr. Sweeting was very understanding. Edward asked if there was anything else that could be done. She said she would reconvene the team, take another look at my films, and see if there was any other way to approach this. I sniffled my way out of the office to wait for my next appointment.

When I next met with my surgeon, she said they had reevaluated my case and that she felt like she could try a different approach. She would try for a lumpectomy followed by chemotherapy and then radiation. If she determined after taking a look inside that a lumpectomy was not feasible, she would not wake me up for permission. She would proceed with the mastectomy. Also, the chemo regimen would change to two chemo drugs instead of four, but I would have to go every week instead of every three weeks! Well, there you have it—a game plan in place. Okay, let's get to it.

The surgery was scheduled quickly, but first, I had to go to a chemo class. If you ever want to scare the daylights out of somebody, send them to a chemo class! Maybe we ought to threaten criminals with chemo. This would certainly cut down on crime! I had no idea about how many chemo drugs there are, how many different side effects there are, or even how many different types of breast cancers there are.

After they had sufficiently scared me straight, I prepared for surgery. I had to buy front-closing soft sports bras to wear after the surgery. I also had to do a thorough deep-cleaning of my home since chemo strips your body of all immunities. This meant carpets, curtains, blinds, windows, and everything else. I also had two long-haired large-breed dogs who lived in my house. If pets live in your home, there is no way to be free of pet dander. I had to ask my friend Jennifer if they could stay with her family until I could bring them back home. I love my dogs, and this was very hard. I cried a river when I had to drop them off. I would ride out to Jennifer's house on Sundays. She has a beautiful climate-controlled indoor kennel. I would sit in a chair and visit with Trixie and Puppy until I got tired, and Edward would take me home. It was so hard leaving them each week. It seemed like they did not understand why I wasn't taking them with me. I couldn't wait for the day when I could take me home again.

I have an extreme aversion to needles, so it was nice to learn that my surgeon planned to implant the chemo port while she was doing the cancer surgery. This saved me from one more invasive procedure. Now I was all set. There was nothing left but to do it. Here we go.

CHAPTER 5

I have always been hard to revive after anesthesia, and this time was no exception. When I was finally able to wake up enough to think, the first thing I did was check to see if both of the "girls" were still there. They were. Whew! My doctor came in to tell me that she was certain she was able to remove all the calcifications, but chemo would make certain of it. She also let me know that the protocol for a lumpectomy requires radiation as well, so there was no way around that.

To be honest, the pain was manageable, but I slept a lot. I felt very relieved to have this part over with. I tried not to dwell on my situation but to constantly thank God for things going as well as they did. My mental health seemed to be in a good place so far. Edward was my constant companion, so I felt like I had someone there to help me. I also had a myriad of family and friends checking in on me. Little did I know that all of that was about to be tested when this chemo journey started.

Let me just say I wouldn't wish chemo on a woman who cheated with my husband! Well, maybe on her but not on anyone else. Chemo ought to cure cancer and a whole lot of other stuff because it wreaks havoc on the body! Between the nausea, mood swings, and hair loss, there are a number of other issues that will just unexpectedly show up out of nowhere for no good reason. It may be neuropathy, joint pains, or stomach issues. You name it. I don't think anybody knows everything that chemo does to the human body.

Chemo said, "I plan to camp out in your body and make your life absolutely miserable until I decide to let go."

I said, "Chemo, you are a liar, and your hair is nappy!"

And then the fight started.

CHAPTER 6

This journey with chemo was both frightening and enlightening. It was terrifying to have to get this poison injected into my body every Friday, but it was enlightening too. I learned so much about cancer, chemo, the human body, and human resolve. I met many women who were paddling their own breast cancer boats, each in their own way. I met very brave women who were dealing with this for the second, and some for the third, time. My mind would not allow me to even think about having to undergo this battle more than once. I learned that each woman's journey is individual to her. We can be a source of encouragement for one another, but each woman deals with it in her own way.

I have had a couple of friends die as a result of breast cancer. I never allowed myself to entertain that as my outcome. It was important to me that I maintained a positive attitude and focused on my faith. I also happened to be working with an amazing group of people at that time. Keeping an area clean and disinfected was important because chemo depletes your immune system, and you are susceptible to most anything. I came in at 9:00 a.m. The young lady who came in early every day made sure that the office was totally disinfected daily! She made sure people sanitized their hands when they came in. This was before COVID-19! We went through Lysol and Clorox wipes like crazy. I will be forever grateful to her for her efforts to protect me.

I also had two bosses. One prayed for me constantly and always made sure I knew I did not have to come in if I didn't feel well. My other boss was my bodyguard. His mother was also experiencing her own cancer battle at the time. I think that made him a little more protective of me. He made sure I had what I needed to be comfortable at work and let me know that I could leave and go home whenever I didn't feel well. I was a contract employee at the time. They could have very easily said, "Thank you, but we will find someone else since you can't be here 100 percent." They never did and were very supportive every step of the way.

I did not take this for granted. I showed up sometimes even when I didn't feel well. I figured that if I was going to not feel well at home, I might as well not feel well at work and get paid for it! It also occurred to me that this was one more example of God's goodness. If I hadn't had this job at the time, I imagine it would have been harder to stay focused and positive; I would've had too much time to wallow in self-pity. No, I'm not trying to sound like a martyr. The reality for many women experiencing this breast cancer journey is that mental health is as much a part of this fight as physical health.

For example, knowing I was going to have to face the world wearing a wig for the first time in my life was daunting. However, I have always been the type of person who felt that if I looked my best, I performed my best. I always used this approach during my professional life. Whenever I had to make an important presentation or had to perform in a work assessment or training, I would make sure that I dressed to feel as professionally confident as possible. I don't wear a full face of makeup every day, but with this journey, it was important to me that I continued to get my nails done and wear my lipstick. This helped me feel as "normal" as possible under the circumstances.

I also met a darling young lady who was so sweet and thoughtful. She was a hairstylist. She would hand-make my wigs and come to my house to do the fittings. She made sure that I had at least two so I could change when one needed styling. To give me an extra boost of confidence, she also would do my eyebrows and eyelashes when I felt well enough.

CHAPTER 7

Let's talk about the financial impact of this nightmare. Even though I was working at the time, I was retired from AT&T after thirty-two years of service. I had retiree health insurance, but I now know how families can be left broke, bankrupt, or financially devastated when facing a catastrophic medical condition. There was surgery, chemo, radiation, prescriptions, and unlimited doctor visits. There were X-rays, MRIs, and ultrasounds. I had to see different doctors for different side effects, like my neuropathy. The bills kept coming, and they were overwhelming.

I felt fortunate to have insurance, but it was just a drop in the bucket. However, I was thankful that insurance covered any of it. I can remember times in my life when I was broker than the Ten Commandments! I couldn't make a flea a wrestling jacket if they were selling gingham for a penny a yard! So it was a blessing to know that insurance would help, and I was able to set up a payment plan to make monthly payments.

As I have mentioned, mental health is a part of this journey, and I'm sure stressing over medical bills would not bode well for a positive mental health experience. It may also be beneficial to see a therapist during this time. Whatever support a woman needs at this time should be sought. Sometimes it's a professional therapist, and sometimes it is talking with another woman who has been through this. Whatever it looks like for each woman, she should be sure to make it a part of the journey.

CHAPTER 8

This journey taught me many life lessons. One is that you find out who your friends are when your boat gets a hole in it. I was both surprised and disappointed by the people who did and did not show up during this experience. However, the one and only person I really needed during this time was God, and he never failed me. I spent a great deal of time praying. I prayed for myself, but I also prayed for all the other women I met and saw regularly at the oncology center.

I need to mention that I am very grateful for all the people I dealt with in this oncology center. It is vitally important for women going through this experience to feel safe and cared for when undergoing chemo. All of these nurses were phenomenal! I had problems having my port accessed. Remember the port whisperer? She came to my rescue again. As it turned out, my port was deeply embedded, so the needles they were trying to use were not long enough. After being jabbed and dug into repeatedly, she realized this and had them change the needle size.

She also told me it was perfectly okay to mention this change each week that I came since there would probably be a different nurse each time, just in case they didn't know they needed to use a longer needle. It would save me some agony.

I remember my first chemo experience. It was a small single cubicle with a very comfortable recliner, a TV, snacks, a warm blanket if I wanted it, and socks for my feet if I wanted them. Then in came all the needles! I had a wonderful nurse that day, named Terri. I have an extreme aversion to needles and started to hyperventilate. She immediately recognized my panic and asked me if I wanted to have Ativan to calm my anxiety. I said yes gratefully. Thank you, Lord, for Ativan! She told me I could ask for it each time I came to help me through this experience, and I did! I was a drowsy, wobbly mess after my chemo was over, but I was not climbing the walls in hysterics.

I had one nurse who would mail me a card of encouragement each week after my chemo when she was my nurse. The port whisperer would stroll through occasionally just to check to be sure everything was going okay for me. I had one nurse who would access my port each week. This was extremely painful, as I have mentioned. She gave me a numbing cream and clear port covers to apply before I came. I was told to apply it thirty minutes before I arrived. This did not help. It was still painful.

She said, "Try applying it forty-five minutes before."

It was still painful.

Finally, she said, "Try one hour before."

This turned out to be the sweet spot, and it helped my anxiety over having my port accessed.

She was also the oncology lab's comedian. Every week, there was something funny in her office. I remember that around Halloween, she had these two skeletons dressed in wedding attire. She also had these skeleton dogs, and she asked her patients to name them.

I endured this chemo experience for months on end. The bright spot was that I never, ever worried about having an unpleasant interaction with anyone working there. This included everyone from the check-in desk to check-out. When I completed my treatment, I wrote a letter to the director of nursing oncology to thank them for this experience and let them know how important it is for people facing cancer and chemo to be treated by caring, conscientious nurses and staff. That part, Vanderbilt got very right.

Chapter 9

Once I was finished with chemo, it was on to radiation. I learned that there is no way around radiation if you have had a lumpectomy. Radiation is part of the lumpectomy protocol. This experience was not painful, just exasperating. I had to go to the hospital every day, Monday through Friday, for four weeks! My appointment was at the same time every day, so I went on my lunch hour. I became very familiar to the valet parking staff. After a while, I would get "How are you today, Ms. Williams?"

The first day did not go as planned. The machine didn't cooperate, and we could not get it done that day. I came back the next day. Guess what? Yep! The dang machine could not read what I needed to have done. With radiation, they make what looks like a cast of the part of your body that will need to undergo the radiation therapy. For whatever reason, the mold they made for me was not connecting to the machine. I had to reschedule again. The next time, it was perfect.

The radiation staff was amazing. They apologized profusely for not being able to get it right at first and took great pains to make the experience as pleasant as possible. Every day, I got a chance to pick the music I wanted to hear while I was being fried. I got a kick out of shocking my staff. One day, I would pick Josh Groban, and the next day, I asked for Meatloaf's "Bat Out of Hell"! The next day, it would be gospel music, and the day after that, it would be Fleetwood Mac. One day, I even cracked them up when I asked for Prokofiev's "Symphony No. 5." That one floored them and was good for a laugh. They would make guesses on what kind of music I would request each day. It became a fun game to think up shocking musical selections each day.

I mentioned that the radiation treatment was not painful, but it was not without its discomforts. Radiation basically burns through your skin. I had to apply a heavy topical ointment several times a day to try to prevent blistering. It made wearing a bra uncomfortable because of chafing. Where I experienced blistering, I had to try to find creative ways of padding with gauze to minimize the irritation. I had to walk around for several days being a greasy mess. I felt like fried chicken! When I finished, my body was two different colors. I was medium rare on one side and medium well on the other side.

Next up, physical therapy. During surgery, Dr. Sweeting removed lymph nodes from under my left armpit to test. This was to determine if the cancer had spread to my lymph nodes. Thank God the answer was no, but it meant that I could not raise my left arm. It was so stiff and tight I thought I would never be able to raise my arm over my head again. Well, there went my pole-dancing career! The physical therapy started out very rough. The exercises they put me through were as hard as Chinese arithmetic! I wasn't sure it was going to work at all, and some days, I wasn't even sure it was worth it. However, I kept going and gradually started to feel the tendons loosen a bit.

Today I can even do jumping jacks, but it took almost a year before I could manage to raise my arm over my head without pain. All in all, I thank God that I am even able to do it at all. God still amazes me every day. I am thankful for healing and don't take it for granted.

CHAPTER 10

Through it all, God's grace and mercy kept me. With his blessings, I was able to endure all that I experienced during this ordeal. I was also thankful that my sweet country man stuck by my side. Eventually, he asked, and I answered. Yep! We were getting married. Planning a wedding while concluding this cancer journey was a pleasant diversion. I'm sure I could have made it through this nightmare without him, but I am certainly grateful that I didn't have to.

I promised myself that going forward, I would not be as obstinate about my health as I was in the past. After all, I am convinced that is how I got here. However, I am still adamant about not just blindly being medically obedient. After my regimen was completed, I was told that I needed to take this "chemo pill" for five years. I tried it for about a month. Taking this medication felt like someone struck a match inside me and set me on fire, and I couldn't put it out! Because it was determined that my cancer was hormone-driven, I could never take any type of hormone-replacement supplement ever again. So this unbearable, incessant, unrelenting hot-flash lifestyle I was now being forced into was not working for me. I would be so hot I would be nauseated. When I went back for my next appointment, I told them that I believed them when they said I was cancer-free, and I was believing God by faith that I was healed, so I would not be taking this "chemo pill." I got the standard "It is for your own good" speech, but I held my ground.

I continued to go for my annual mammograms and my follow-up oncology appointments each year. Six years later, I have exceeded my five-year cancer goal and continue to be cancer-free. Remember earlier how I said I believe that God allows things to happen in my life that I am either supposed to learn something from or do something with? This is no exception. Since my journey, I have been asked several times to speak to different groups about my experience, especially in October, when we acknowledge Breast Cancer Awareness Month. I have also known several women personally who have been going through their own breast cancer journey. I have taken what I learned and experienced to share with and encourage other women on the journey. I have had other people contact me and ask if I would talk to their friend or family member about my experience or share information with them.

For example, you would be surprised at the number of women who either weren't told or just forgot that they would need to get soft, no underwire, front-closing bras for after their lumpectomy surgeries. I also try to share information about the permanent hair loss that the drug Taxotere causes. Whether or not a woman includes it in her treatment is up to her and her medical team. However, I do know that some women are not being told about this upfront.

I'll also share my own secret nausea remedy. I'm from Alabama, and when we were kids, our moms used to give us a drink called Buffalo Rock ginger ale if they thought we were coming down with measles because if you drink it heated up, it would make the bumps pop right out. If we had an upset stomach, our moms would get us to sip this really strong ginger ale to settle our stomachs. Buffalo Rock is distributed by the Buffalo Rock Bottling Company. The recipe was created during the Civil War and was used on the battlefield for medicinal purposes. I was given two different nausea medications. I never took either of them. I managed my nausea by drinking Buffalo Rock. I have recommended this to several other women, and remarkably, they all report that this drink is amazing for managing nausea.

Once I hit my five-year cancer-free mark, my friends and I who have had our own journeys decided to do a "Fight Like a Girl" photo shoot. This was very empowering, and we had a blast sharing this together.

I try to be an encouraging voice for other women experiencing breast cancer. Recently, one of my friend's sisters-in-law started her breast cancer journey. I text with her and encourage her regularly. Her faith is strong, and she is very positive. I encouraged her to do her own photo shoot when she completes her journey. To encourage her, I mailed her my pink boxing gloves to use in her photo shoot. I hope she will and then pass them on to encourage another sister in the struggle.

I am thankful to God for his healing mercies, but I am also thankful that he is using me to help support other women through their own journeys. I still believe that cancer can be cured, but until the powers that be decide to, I will stay on the battlefield, encouraging and supporting other women in whatever way I can.

Oh yeah, one last thing. I believe that people come into our lives for a reason, a season, or a time. I am not sure why Edward came into my life. I believed it was forever. Unfortunately, it was just for a time. I am still grateful for the kindness he showed me during this ordeal.

About the Author

Cheryl Williams is a first-time author. She holds several degrees including a master's degree in organizational management. She has one daughter, Veronica, and one grand angel, Adriana. She is a breast cancer survivor who is often asked to make speaking appearances on the subject. She has also donated a kidney to one of her sorority sisters and is an advocate for living donors. She is a member of Alpha Kappa Alpha Sorority, Inc.

Milton Keynes UK
Ingram Content Group UK Ltd.
UKHW030306301024
450168UK00021B/18